In the Empire
of Chimeras

Also by Martin Anderson

Poetry

The Kneeling Room *
The Ash Circle *
Heard Lanes
Dried Flowers
Swamp Fever
The Stillness of Gardens
Black Confetti
Belonging *
Snow. Selected Poems 1981–2011 *
Interlocutors of Paradise
The Lower Reaches *
Obsequy for Lost Things *
Ice Stylus *

Prose

The Hoplite Journals (complete in one volume) *

The Hoplite Journals I-XXIX *
The Hoplite Journals XXX-LIX *
The Hoplite Journals LX-LXXIX *

An asterisk denotes a Shearsman title.

In the Empire of Chimeras

Martin Anderson

Shearsman Books

First published in the United Kingdom in 2018 by
Shearsman Books
50 Westons Hill Drive
Emersons Green
BRISTOL
BS16 7DF

Shearsman Books Ltd Registered Office
30–31 St. James Place, Mangotsfield, Bristol BS16 9JB
(this address not for correspondence)

www.shearsman.com

ISBN 978-1-84861-616-5

ACKNOWLEDGEMENTS
These poems, a substantial number under different titles, were first
published by the University of the Philippines Press in 1999, in the
collection *Black Confetti*. All have been revised. Many extensively.
In their revised form they articulate and bring into greater clarity
and relief that original focus and vision which animated them.

Contents

"In the circle beginning and end are the same."

—Heraclitus

De las Islas e Indios

In sea wind their basilicas rot.
Their porticos crumble. The courtyards
of their lichened mansions thicken.
In our dark faces they stained the pale lineage
of their blood. Up long alluvial shores
of the coast they entered, through a
humid half-light of mosquitoes and dust,
scabbards interleaved with prayer.
Over their wide piazzas vespers rang:
we practiced writing the names they gave us
in a language not ours. In the warm seas
of our archipelago we stood, looking west
ward. Upon sweating abutment
and plinth, across hot esplanades, a red dusk
moved. Slowly. The *guayabana* ripened,
year in year out. On each pensile
stem, tilted escritura, the angel
of fecundity stood, blowing, blowing.
Until, with *bayabas*, it was restored.

Flight

(*IM* N.V.M. Gonzalez)

Within this cooling swathe of light, the earth's unwrapped.
A rush of wind on a white wing.
Ascending, out of the path of something
hard and true, something immeasurably dense and rich,
into what? Beneath us, San Fernando glares
under a tropical noon, clearly laid out rooftops and walls, a grid
of streets transfixed; sharded light lifts up from them.
On one side, the sea's wrinkled integument,
brilliant strip of calcined sand; far out
umber of coral, water bruised to a deeper tint
of itself. On the other, as we tilt, following us,
narrating our journey, the high green of the Cordillera
lush in drifting cloud, pines gripping
in cold wind off each ridge, a silent geography
where water pours thousands of feet through air without a sound.
You look down, upon a road of moving palms.
A tricycle weaving through its cloud of dust.
A carinderia. A clump of banban. The land: spread out
beneath you. Caught there, in the stubborn terrain
of the senses, it had burned day after day, year after
year since you left, or did not leave; fashioning a voice
in which it might co-exist with that image of itself
you had taken with you and were impatient to reclaim.

A House on Remedios Street

Where the gutter flows with a viscid white suspension,
through the long hot shadows of the evening.
Above steps, the oily penumbra of a lamp is thrown
outwards. A brackish emanation floats among the flower
pots, the ghostly breath of a dried out mangrove
in gardens, lingers, wet upon the arms, the
impress of a dying osculation. A streak of fragrance
where the hairpins dropped, is gathered now,
on the curbside's quiet, where the cambered dark runs
into the trees, small airborne fires, *ignes fatui*,
hover. And small boys, following them, leaping
to cup that luminous particle in their hands.
Across the broken sidewalk, comes the soft rapid flutter
of a fan, followed by its shadow, and the long
inhaled breath of an ageing matrona at the top
of the steps, smoking a cigarette, lost in contemplation.

On an Unnamed Avenue at Evening

Through the heavy roar of traffic
a note, chord – heard/unheard – fading somewhere
beyond the lamp's glow, where your arm
is buried in shadow. Irrepressible music,
rhythm, that our lives make, tracking us through
each day, hour, minute. Our fate prescribed.
You hear it. A silent concatenation in the evening
upon railing and step. The dark ripples
against your body for a moment, washes
through you with its inaudible vibration.
You lean your head back, and inhale
the dank odour stirred by the fan
then walk over to the window and lay your hands
upon the sill. An almost imperceptible rhythm runs
through them. Between each surge, phantoms
crowd round you. Hopes, ambitions,
illusions. Then they drift up, like smoke. You stand
at the window as it darkens. And listen.

The Amanuensis

Through the obfuscated lines of her life
she walks. The darkness under her eyes like an ink
that's dried on a faded message.
Someone is there, in the narrow
room, in the clear light of her retinas, scribbling.
A treatise, on who she is. She hears,
from time to time, their faint sound, like a bird
scratching at a pane. Then, it ceases.
In the broken dream of transparency, her hand
searches for a hand. Amidst the dream's
overlapping voices she hears her words,
again, coming back to her,
as if from the ghost of a life
through which she walked. Beside a courtyard
of dust and ragged palms, she pauses. And listens.
Questioning who it is, who
makes her speak through the enveloping night
on the unmarked street. And through yesterday's
rain she hears the long slow whistle
of the train as it is departing
for a country without names. And the sound of
her feet stumbling, again
and again, through the hot night after it.

Dusk

"But at my back…"
—Andrew Marvell

Over the linens of cheap rundown pensions, with their
threadbare insignias of unknown lives, the satyric gaze
of the mortuary cosmeticist roams. Within the
blue twilight that seeps through alleyways it floats
into deep swaying stems of cogon grass, where a dog
suckles its litter and a woman raises her thighs, into
the opulent condominiums of Makati; then out
over banana plants by railroad tracks where it steals
through huts of the poor entering their dreams, to pause
in the green mansions of Forbes Park. By Canal de la
Reina, by roofs of tin and floor-planks on tottering
stilts, home to crude wood totems of the Virgin,
clumsily carved Christs, it rests. Returning home
a manicurist from a beauty parlour anxiously intones
a Paternoster. Behind her, in the window of a drab pension,
a spider climbs. A *VACANCIES* sign bends and fades in
fierce heat. Above it hangs a dark debellishment of flies.

To Every Window

Hot air, blowing through corridors, stairwells
and on landings. Odour of sweat and sampaguita.
The ephemeral music of bars. Through the gutted
heart of the Pension Casa Blanca charcoal drifts,
powdering the weeds in spectral yards.
Behind them itinerant musicians sing
beside the deserted underpasses of the city.
Night carries the weight of their song to every window.
God Is Love, in huge bold letters, stares from
a jeepney. A blue, electric light floats over
Ermita. In the shadows, rats. The sound of voices
that don't know whether to agree or contend.
Invisible lives. In the soft glaze of her eyes a liminal light.
Scraps of memory. Incomplete biography. They turn
into a dark alleyway. He presses his cheek into the hollow
of her cheek. Nothing. Only, in her
austere smile, the inclement emptiness of the night.

Nightsong

Night's fragments caught in the eddy of air
from the open window: thin residue of diesel
from a parking lot, jigsaw of voices, odour
of a flower I cannot name. Your dark heart beating beside
me to the throb of a generator behind the trees.
In the sultry air straining, manufacturing its dreams.
The ambient glow from a street light falls onto the floor.
In the gloom of the dresser table mirror, half in shadow,
I can almost see your face, its gentle lineaments
of mouth and nose. Somewhere, from within the
Circle, the strains of a lost childhood rehearsing itself
on a piano cross the courtyard and enter the
window; and your hand grips tightly, in sleep, mine.

The Home of Pain

"In Rusafa I came upon a palm…
  I said: you stand alone, like me so far from home."
      —Abd al-Rahman

The world goes on and on, transforming itself.
Memory sings day after day, excavating the secret
repositories of hope and despair. Over the road Ospital ng
Maynila tops its drive of tattered palms, a thin stream
of antiseptic wafting through its open wards out into
night-time traffic. The water in the bay lapping steps
arrives at the end of its long journey. Our dubieties
multiply. In the crowded forecourt of the mind
what image is enjoined, to which we defer: whiter than
sheets, cooler than ice? Let us reach over and touch
it before the day, choked with equivocations and lies,
dissolves it. Or is it only another tattered palm, tearing
in turbulent air, waving the soot of its striated shadow
before us; a dream, rooting and uprooting itself
in the rubble of a past it cannot remember, or forget; but
to which it is condemned, endlessly, to keep returning.

The Garden

"Yea are like unto whited sepulchres, which indeed appear beautiful out-
ward, but within are full of dead men's bones and of all uncleanness."
                                        —Matthew 23:27

Beyond the crumbling statuary of cement,
flyover, pedestrian bridge, water tower,
behind the walls of a derelict dark garden
there is a pool of healing grey water, that glows.
Asphalt run-off, dew; impure elixir of the night
made clear again among contorted
petals, riot of shadow, where the twisted iron
of a gatepost knots the leafage of an almost
extinguished fragrance. Drink here, in the dust
of this silence, within the walls, this slow
sad evaporant of the moon. And savour, for one
moment, before you pass, what rises before you
in the dusk; familiar ghost, crepuscular face
of inarticulate longing, torn out of the earth
from such a depth that even the yawning stench
of the roadside drains away before it.

Remedios Circle

On this hot night, in this circle of stone and worn grass,
by the gates of dilapidated mansions, friends, families saunter
from stifling shacks, children romp under streetlights,
vendors rest their push-carts on curbs. Behind glass
and hanging plants, in air conditioned draught, waiters yawn.
The end of day. Uncontaminated memories float
with the scent of the pomelo tree, over weed-strewn lots
and sluggish esteros. Over lichened stone angels,
over broken balustrades and marble fonts. The leaves
of the santol tree shine under the moon. We stroll down
a road that's quiet, unillumined. The dead gases of the city
hover above our heads. A jeepney stops by us. The
scuffed toe of someone's shoe traces an incomplete
circle, amid husks and scattered rinds, upon the floor.

The Kiss

"You're afraid the kiss might betray you
   to other beds now of the past
   which nevertheless could haunt you."
                    —George Seferis

Now sleep has robbed her make up
of its lustrous glow. Upon
her pillowed head the night
breathes noisily. She does not stir.
In the unrobed dark of her skin he inhales
a shadowy crucible of old intimacies
a fragrance, an unexhumed sweetness
of journeys commenced, unforetold
destinations. Confused, he spends the night
looking for her. Amid the ruined
images of day he finds her, pensive,
sad, as if she had come back
to a room she needed to recompose,
imperfectly remembered. On her ankles
and feet a dusty, phosphorescent pallor,
as from wild untramped roads, lingers.
And doubt, scavenging her face
for something that is not there.

Remains

As if her hands were suspended in a gesture
of adoration: the inscrutable shadows of her
being furled around her. He bends over her body;
tries to think. Fragments: a lost
conversation. Silence... augury
of lies. He follows clues, tries to
elicit from her face the obscure
purposes of her heart: hands
clasped in front of her, perhaps,
in ritual scourging; or the simple
economics of predation? Either way
he knows her kind did not bury its dead
with flowers. And the dark bolus,
within the chest, she died of was not grief.
Shoes, neatly folded panties and socks
arranged beside her. A heart atrophied, puckered.
Suffused through it, like thickening cloud,
that long grey sediment of her life
through which she moved: her footprints,
preserved in it, echo. Yield only
a sieving of hints and whispers, an expired
dream amid a tumulus of shadows.

The Quay

The heart stands in a flux of shadow, pushing, beating
against the quiet of a wave that breathes the immense
emptiness of quays. There they recollect, in the dark
water, the flickering names of all the places that have
diverted them *guava groves at the edge of town fragrant*
in night air seas deep and precarious as time
the blandishments, and the dalliances. Pharmacies
and backstreets in the heat and dust of cities where
daily they listened to voices of imprecation and bravura
in innumerable bars. Counting the hours, inhaling the
odour of carbolic in cheap pensions, until the expiry of
their visas. And, at night, in endless inventories of their
insomnia etched onto the wall, places their hands could reach
out and touch. Drifting, drifting, on a sea which, they knew,
would always bring them back to the pandemonium of
quays. From which they would inevitably, again, set out.

Spring, the Return

Chatter of chemical codes among the trees. Language
of arrival and departure. Like migrating birds, names in the air.
                                                          People,
places. Undeclared itineraries. Voices drifting across estuaries, roads
dusty with the feet of a procession under agoho trees.
Across stairwells fresh with the odour of jasmine after a death,
rooms stale with the air of connubial evenings. TV sets
left on all night. Messages unanswered. A door, closing.
And the mind always coming back, being's insomnia, to this
thin revenant of light upon the floor, pulse of the present and
the future, to the heart's incoherence, its unappeasable shadow.